A Long Way From Essex

Doug Gregory is a member of Sandwriters Inc., a writers group based in Goolwa, South Australia. Sandwriters publish the journal *Speak Out* annually, which includes selected works by its members plus contributions from other writers and artists. To purchase copies of Doug's previous books and past and current editions of *Speak Out*, direct enquiries to Sandwriters, PO Box 56, Goolwa, South Australia 5214.

Also by Doug Gregory

Bindies Only Tickle (1999)
A Candle For Tomorrow (2005)
Where Are the Angels (2015)
Night Café and other poems (2016)

Doug Gregory

A Long Way From Essex

Acknowledgements

'Seven Shades of Grey' and 'My Sweet Lord' were selected for inclusion in *Speak Out* 2018 edition.

A Long Way From Essex
ISBN 978 1 76041 681 2
Copyright © Doug Gregory 2019

First published 2019 by
GINNINDERRA PRESS
PO Box 3461 Port Adelaide 5015 Australia
www.ginninderrapress.com.au

Contents

Averages	9
Baiting and Waiting	12
Thank You Thank You	13
Seven Shades of Grey	15
A Day After Dying	16
The Broken Marriage	17
George and the Generation Gap	19
Coffee Card	21
Wrecked at Harold Hill, Essex	23
Weddings and Funerals	26
The Lonely Sun	30
This Day	31
The Christmas Cringe	32
Cliché Not Dinkum	34
Beauty	35
Gods and Dogs	37
Common Ground	38
Good Old-fashioned Romance	39
None the Wiser	40
Gaye's Outburst	42
The New Rev	46
Just Thinking	48
The Gaming Room	50
My Kind of Hell	52
Sorry	55
Frozen	56
Now He's Gone	57
Memories	59
The Operating Theatre	60
DV	62

Not Making Sense	64
Home and Away	65
Urban Bourbon and Beer	67
Things I'll Never Know	69
Sebastian	71
Sarah Ann	74

Hit Parade 77

My Sweet Lord	79
If Not For You	81
Avalanche	83
Stop	85
The Other Guy	86
Honesty	87
Yesterday	89
Another Tear Falls	90
Waiting for the Miracle	92
Little Things	94
Liar Liar	96
Hit and Miss	98
Good Vibrations	99
I Should Have Known Better	101
Alone Again Or	102
I Love You Because	104

Dedicated to the memory of
Sarah Ann (1931–2017)

We're all equal…
as each of us finds out
(*Seven Shades of Grey*)

Averages

My mate Will is
An averages man
The law of averages
He applies it to everything
He tells me,
'We live for about…
Thirty thousand days.'
Sounds a lot different
To eighty years
One moment sounding like
Forever
Until one does the sums
At 68
I've already had twenty-five thousand!
And days pass
Very quickly.

He bombards me with
Statistics and projections
How certain it is that
Because THIS occurs
THAT will follow, and so on.
He says it's balance.

Will is an average kind of man
Lives an average life
In an average kind of place
A gated village
For the over sixty-fives.
He says,
'No one there realises
The life they have left
Is just days
They do nothing with them
Sit around
Waiting for that final day
They see life
Looking from behind their see-through curtains'
Which he observes
Blowing in the breath.

He says,
'It all averages out
So much per cent of this
So much per cent of that
The average man
Has his share
Of good days and
Bad days
He'll have
So many wins
So many losses
You can't defy it
Can't deny it.'

I enjoy discussing philosophy with my mates.

This is…
The most scintillatingly fascinating
Boring and
A tad disturbing
Piece of information
Anyone has ever given me.
Fatalistic, though consoling
Confronting, though thought-provoking
Encouraging and inevitable
Sobering.

Will says,
'If today's a shit of a day
Don't dwell on it
The averages say
A good day is due.
Look back on your life
And see how the good
Followed bad
And the bad followed good.
Let the averages
Have their way
And don't resist.'

I went home
And thought about it.
Of course, he's right.
At 77
Will's got a thousand days left.

Baiting and Waiting

Sometimes I think about
The carnage I cause
To the parallel
Miniature
World
And the power
We have over it.

I place the baits
Amongst the often crumbs strewn area
Around the bread bin.
I occasionally observe
As the industrious, loyal to their queen, ants
Dutifully take the offering
Return to camp
And thus wipe out
The whole colony.

I'm never quite sure I should feel
Clever and self-satisfied
That I've fixed a problem.

Would I do this
Were it to be reported on the news
With graphic zoomed in pictures
Of the suffering
Or
Maybe
Think of a way
We could live in this world together.

Thank You Thank You

Thank you
Mate
The unknown guy who
Stepped between me and some thug who
Wanted to smash my face
Many years ago.

Thank you
To the unknown pilot
Who steered my dodgy
Air India plane to safety
A month later
It came down in a jungle.

Thank you
To my second girlfriend's father
Who consoled me
When I was inconsolable
After she didn't want me any more.

Thank you to
The mindless moron
Who reminded me
Of how I once
May have appeared
Drunk in public.

Thank you to my wife
For making me realise that
Wanting to get drunk every night
Had no future.

Thank you
To Arthur Lee
He first awakened
The compassion in me.

Thank you to Ron
Who helped me to see
That in the office there's more to life
Than gossip and tea.

Thank you to my first love
A lifelong friendship
She has gifted me.

And,
Thank you to all the gods
Who have determined that
I'm not worthy
Of contacting
And
Accordingly
Not condemned me to live
In a fantasy world.

Seven Shades of Grey

Many good old pals
Are facing the ultima
We're all equal
As each of us find out.

Pierre says bugger it all
Just gonna do what I like to do

Sally takes a different view, one day at a time
One day crying, the next with a smile

Harold is an optimist
Fearing the worst but planning ahead

Terry is a mystery
Still has his cigarettes between
Chemotherapy

Johno is a total wreck
Keeps crashing down, hitting the deck

Poor old Robbie is concerned only about looks
He's abandoned his philosophy, music and books

And jolly old Kim
Thinks it'll all work out
Has a drink and a laugh
Nothing ever bothers him.

Whilst I
With the same total years behind
Count my blessings
Keep a good heart
And consider my next gamble.

A Day After Dying

So,
What the fuck was that all about!
Ducking and diving
Deceiving and lying
Believing, denying
Laughing and crying
All the heartache
The pain
The losses, the gains
It all came and went
Like an express train.

Where to now?
There's nothing around
Not a sky, not a ground
Not even a sound.

So, what on earth was that all about
Everything's gone
It's come to the end
Nothing here to protect
Nothing left to defend
It's over, it's out
The end of the bout.

The Broken Marriage

A life in the new world
Was never something
I thought I could sustain
Feeling foreign
Talking different
In the sun
Over and over again.

You took me to places
The outback places
To sing with strangers around an old gum tree
Said this is the life, the open spaces
You'll never feel more free.

I covered up my truth, you know
And have a-many
Pangs of guilt
Freedom for me
Was never open spaces
Or strangers, new people
In all your favoured places.

I started longing
For the old familiar streets
Cosy pubs and cold dark nights
For bookshops with
A big poetry section
Spent much time drifting
In reflection.

You loved me for
What you thought I was
Or what you thought I'd be
But I only ever lived for the day
The future, never a part of me.

Now I can put it
All into words
I didn't know how to say it then
And I'll always have
The pangs of guilt
For not saying
What I meant.

George and the Generation Gap

In my lifetime
The generation gap
Was never wider
Than during the 'hippie' years.
The late 1960s were filled with
Social revolution
A new culture
And the youth were calling it.

In my private world
I played my part.
I was fortunate to have
A friend from
The ageing generation
A man of 30 or so more years of life
Than me.
On the surface
We showed little appreciation
For the vastly differing views
We each held.
Me
And my like minded companions
Would spout our radical, fanciful ideas
Of a new world emerging.
My friend George
Would ridicule them
With laughter, a 'listen to this' Dean Martin song and
'have another drink'.

George loved life
Enjoyed the social occasion
Embraced the company of
Me and my companions
And with warmth and generosity
Bridged the generation gap
Like no one else I knew.
George made one laugh
And feel welcomed
To the older generation
Like no one I ever knew.

To the memory of George.

Coffee Card

There's an elderly guy
I pass most mornings
Sitting at the edge of an outdoor area
Of a local café
His motorised wheelchair stationed nearby.
He's been there for months
Every day
Dressed in raggedy clothes
Looks like a war veteran
A Vietnam vet perhaps
And poverty stricken
Though a bit presumptuous to
Judge by appearance.

Always alone
I feel inclined to drop him my change
Or even a crisp fifty-dollar note.
He gestures in a very friendly manner
Towards me, and my dog
And watches intently if I leave my dog tied to a post
Whilst I pop to the shop next door
And delights upon seeing me return
My dog wagging her tail, ecstatic to see me again
He appears to cherish the reunion
Of me and my dog.

I strike up a brief
Good Morning conversation with him
'Enjoying your coffee?'
He nods, with a
Beaming, toothless smile
I say, 'Do you have a coffee card?'
He shakes his head
Not knowing what the hell I'm talking about
I explain, 'Six coffees and the next one's free'
Five bucks a week he could save
Every other person there, cashed-up
Presents theirs for a stamp or a freebie
And it bothers me that
None of the three staff or manager
Concerned so with their busyness
Has ever thought
To give him
A coffee card.

Wrecked at Harold Hill, Essex

I don't get back to the 'Hill'
Very often
The place I grew up
A place, some would say, is
Rough as guts
Though it wasn't way back then.
For me now
It's the other side of the world
In more ways than one.

I left so long ago
Almost everything
From the time
Is gone.
But the house still stands
Number 47.

On my most recent return
I stood opposite the house
For several minutes
Just gazing.
I saw Dad
Returning on his bicycle from work
I saw Mum tending flowers
Early on a springtime evening
Through an open window I heard
An old hit song by Cliff Richard
On the Decca record player
I saw me, my brother, Mum and Dad, our pet dachshund
Leaving for our summer holiday
On a sunny Saturday morning
And I saw the middle of the night
Christmas Eve, the stocking full of surprises
At the end of my bed.

This is a tear-jerker
Like no other
It leaves me wrecked.

Everything has gone
All the people
The way of living
A sudden onset
Of loss and grieving
The realisation I'll never see it
Never see it again.

I refocus on the house
My old home
Run down
Boarded up
The front garden a crumbling, concreted parking space
My upstairs childhood bedroom
The downstairs family living room
In darkness, in silence.

I have only one final thought
A final wish
That would be for the best
That they bring in the wrecking ball
To lay it all to rest.

Weddings and Funerals

This morning my iPad is
Full of images
Tap to download
A load of snaps
From
Another family wedding.
Of course I wasn't there
Didn't get invited
Didn't want to go
After all…
I live 10,000 miles apart…
A long way from Essex.

Another family wedding
Previously it was a funeral
Before that
More weddings.
The gatherings all look the same
All the fine looking people
In their fine clothes
The strangely familiar settings
The same smiles
Walking down aisles.

The men, the women
Look the same
As in previous bundles of snaps
The new people
Look like the same people
In the snaps
From 1996.
At the funerals
And the weddings
A new generation
Of little ones
Resemble those
Of decades ago.

I haven't been a part of
The scene
For all my adult life
I'm an occasional drop-in
It's all so very
'Where I came from'
And I never wanted
To be there
In the first place.
I was separated at youth
By my own design
Never wanted
To go that way
A family, commitment
Day after day.

I look at these snaps
With a certain degree
Of cringeness, displeasure
For
At times
Following a wedding
Decay sets in
A separation, divorce
A settlement, resentment
Insecure, broken-hearted children.
Following a funeral
Anticipation takes hold
Who gets an inheritance
Who's left out in the cold.

Looking once more
At the snaps
I don't feel jealous
Don't feel left out
Don't feel a part of it
It's not what I'm about
I know that again
Sometime
I'll receive another
Almost identical
Set of pictures
From another wedding or funeral or christening

I return
To my different life and
Whenever they've asked me
'What's so different?'
All I really tell them is
I don't go to weddings and funerals.

The Lonely Sun

It stands supreme
The omnipotent presence
In the sky.

The sun is the visible god
It giveth life
It taketh life
Nothing is eternal
No need to seek an invisible power
It's there for you
Every day
The sun will have
The final say.

The sun is the light, the power
The sun is unapproachable
The veil around us
Protects from its fury
We destroy it…and only then
Will the sun react in anger.

It's there for you
Every day
All powerful
With the final say.

This Day

Nothing doing today
Ordinary
A bit like yesterday
I need to reboot
I'm neglecting too many important things
Been taking it easy, lazy
Don't want any complications
Just afternoon coffee with Susan
Forget what I'm winning and losing
Indulging in silliness with my dog
Whilst slowly accumulating a backlog
Having a quiet glass of wine alone and
Disconnecting my telephone
I been neglecting so much
Like…my new nice friends
My neighbourhood responsibilities
The uncommitted commitments
My health and wellbeing
And my writing…yes, truly
I'm writing this three days into the future.

The Christmas Cringe

It's my 69th Christmas
They just keep coming round
The 3rd or 4th through to
14th, 15th, maybe 18th were greatly anticipated.
Surprises, giving, receiving
Happy families.
Then I came of age
A rot began to set in
A dread
No more surprise, anticipation
It's 'here we go again'
The monstrous commercial
Christmas bandwagon rolls into town.

My good friend in London
A peaceful, loving, humanitarian type
Detests it with some passion
She describes it as,
'Being bombarded with fucking tinsel and lights
All for squeezing as much money from us
To celebrate one day of the year.'

And most people, religious or not, go along with it.

I live in the warm, sunny climate where
Christmas is the middle of summertime.
My friend should try coping with
The tinsel and lights here
'White Christmas' and 'Jingle Bells' blast out
From every shopping precinct
New torturous, awful renditions of these songs
Add to the cringe
Santa Claus walks around in a
Hot red suit on a red hot day
Looking like he's about to explode
And Christmas trees adorn every town centre
Draped with
Look alike snowflakes and coloured balls.

The build up to this one day is weeks, months
From middle of the year onwards
When mince pies and puddings are out to grab your attention.

The world is in turmoil
Millions are homeless and starving
And we, in the first world
In a frenzy of consumerism
Forget about it all.
Let's celebrate!

Cliché Not Dinkum

The dark-skinned
First-time visitor to
The main street roughhouse pub
Had had a gutful
Of snide, offensive comments
Being made by
A local charmer.
Though his mates were calling
Out of order
He persisted.

In defence
Of his racist ranting
The charmer reminded his mates
Of a well known phrase, saying
'What's the matter with you lot
Never heard of
Sticks and stones may break my bones
but words can never
hurt me.'

The wretched recipient of the tirade
Left a half glass of beer and
Walked out
Hurt
With his head down.

Beauty

When our roads first crossed
You were a
Beauty, popularity, pageant queen
Not willingly
But by involuntary inclusion
A seventies workplace thing
I could not see through it
For years
Until one moment arrived
When I offered my congratulations
And your truth burst through.
The image was replaced by
A natural, humble essence of desire.

You've carried it through
For decades since
Always appearing easy
In those awkward situations
Offering generosity and trust
Forgiveness
When the deed was merely a misdemeanour
Staying open
When most would close up.

Your beauty
Puts me in a spin
It never leaves
Never dims
Your eyes direct
Endlessly twinkling
Alive
Your smile
Always honest
Your honesty
Always assured.

How little I knew
Of all of this
Before our roads first crossed.

Gods and Dogs

My neighbour has
Gone to god
In her garden
She's left her dog
To
Terrorise
The
Neighbourhood.

Common Ground

After six years
Of grunts and ignorance
KC and I finally get to talk
We've found common ground.
He's the one at the TAB agency behind the counter
I'm the one who frequents the place
He's the IT freak
I'm the punter.

They're getting 'exciting' brand-new computer machines
And now
He never shuts up.

Never before
A hint
In his eyes
Of invitation, contact
Never a clue
Of amiability
Never any risk
I'd have to share some small talk
But now, he never shuts up.
Most things, I suppose, come to those with patience.

Good Old-fashioned Romance

How would I win her heart
I thought 'hello'
Was a pretty good start
A week later
A sweet, sincere compliment
A week later
We were thrown together
By our work mates
In the bar
In December '79
Sit here, sit there
Not too far apart
Drinks, glances
Snatched moments of conversation and later
A walk on the sand
I held her hand
Then, a suggestion
To go to my house
For coffee
When everything was closed.
She did.

Would I show her my poetry?
I did.
She read it
She got it.

We've been together
Since nineteen seventy-nine.

None the Wiser

This really is a most
Disagreeable situation
Repeated every now and again
My wife and I are treated
To dinner
By a neighbour acquaintance of ours
As payment and reward
For odd jobs I do for him
Nothing too taxing, time consuming or costly
And happy to do it for free.

We meet at 6 p.m.
By 6.05 p.m. I'm willing the clock fast forward
It's just how it is
When one is in the company
Of someone
'not my type of person'.
In that first five minutes
I've thought:
I'll learn nothing new tonight
I'll hear the repeated stories
Of his failing health
The 'I'm not racist but' remarks
About Aboriginals and black South Africans
All the connections he's made in life with
Aristocrats, world-class doctors, army generals and
Other big shots.

My wife sits looking attentive and interested
Saying little
And I will speak only
When I jump in on his pause.

I'll learn nothing new tonight
And he'll be
None the wiser.

Gaye's Outburst

One morning back in the nineties
At breakfast
In the kitchen
Birds singing outside, radio on inside
An intelligent friend of mine, Gaye
Burst out of the blocks with the statement
'If I hear one more fucking report about
Bill Clinton and his prick'
Her voice now raising to nearly its limit
'I'm going to fucking lose it!'

Mildly stung by this outburst
Mainly by her selection of expletives as
Gaye never used foul language
I was holding back giggles
In the presence of her mild-mannered husband Charles
But fully understood her venomous tirade
At the saturation coverage
Of a then current affairs issue.

Gaye was usually quite articulate
Interesting to converse with
Was of an alternative mind and
Had opinions on most things.
But this episode has stuck with me
My respect for her increased a notch.

She was the age I am now
Seventy-ish
And she's still around
So that crisis of the mind didn't finish her off
Though I'm informed
By associates of hers that
Gaye has lost it these days.

For me
I'm driven to distraction frequently
By the same over-enthusiastic media reporters and
Every once in a while
Have to write a verse or two
Hinting at looming madness.

But the thing getting me
Hotter and hotter
Under the collar,
Whilst I'm thinking about
The loss of my mother
As she lives on with dementia
My dog, ageing and sick, needing a visit to the vet
My excruciatingly painful, throbbing, damaged knee
My mate Will talking a lot of crap again
My wife, or was it me, who
Got out the wrong side of the bed today
And arriving at the bank ATM
Without my cash withdrawal card,
Is when I'm asked
Over and over
The same words
With a forced smile and
An expectation of a positive smiling response
By every shop assistant
Council counter officer
The takeaway food guy
The pop-up shop B-grade salesperson
And just about everyone,
'Are you having a good day so far?'

Whatever has happened to people
In the public serving business
Stripped of their uniqueness
By the same staff training blurt.

I decide to leave the shopping mall and think
Just as Gaye did
'If I hear that phrase one more time
I'm going to fucking lose it!'

The New Rev

There's a new guy in town
The Reverend
The new priest
As some call him
Or Father.

I watch him
The revered man
And am puzzled
Wondering what all the fuss is about
All the fuss made of him
All the fuss
Made around his status.

The Reverend shows
An arrogance
Rarely seen around this town
Installed into the nice big comfortable house
On the corner of the park
His very presence
Brings people, metaphorically
To their knees
In order to look
Higher up at him.

I am not cynical
Because of his status
It's just the man and the power and dominance
He cherishes
Over his followers.

The believed wisdom
Truth and answers
He exudes
Is almost visible
But his arrogance and superiority
Ascends above it all.

He likes it at the top
A protected species
Amongst the flock
He enjoys looking down
Having control and
The final say.

I am not a believer
There are countless people
Everywhere
With open minds
And a beautiful take on life
I stand with them.

But
If I were to be
Cajoled
Into thinking
'I've found it'
Would I really want to be taught
Preached and lectured to
By the new Rev?

Just Thinking

I got some solitude
Just hanging around thinking
Like I always do
About life, my life
Feeling that I waste so much.

The men want me to go
Fishing, sailing
Golfing
Join the men's club and build a boat
All the usual things
I don't want to go with the men
I could go and jump
From an aeroplane
Join the conservation group and
Plant trees
Hang out at the bar and
Listen
To the old boys tell
The same old stories.

But I choose to think
And read
And write
And think more
I have fantasies, desires and dreams
Wonder what it would be like
If I won a million bucks
If I lived somewhere else
If my wife left me

If my dog died
If I lost my sight
Or my legs
Or my mind
If my ex turned up
Out of the blue
If I'd mastered the guitar
And become a pop star
And if I'd done
All the things
I said I would do.

There's my mind
There's my body
My mind is overworked
Confused
Worn out
It needs a break
My body's ageing
But can still run
Is underworked
Needs some fun.

I'm thinking,
There'd be nothing better
Than being naked with someone new
If they'd be up for it too.

The Gaming Room

Jackpots up for grabs
At one chance in a million
Irritating jingles and
Non-stop flashing lights
Filtered deodorisers
They come here every night
The losers all together
Sad and lifeless-looking people
The old, near penniless
Or, with a redundancy
A severance payout package to splash
The young, near penniless
Or, with a drug dealing transaction
Pocket full of cash to splash
And the few lively-looking
Couples
With a life
Just something to do
As they're passing through
For twenty minutes or so.

But,
Watch out for the low life
They're after your drop
Your wallet, your jacket, your bag
They won't stop
They're on the lookout
Like a snake
Awake
From its winter slumber
Creeping through the cold desperation
The distracted absent-minded
And crawling through
The warm shadows.

My Kind of Hell

We're off to Bali
For couple of weeks
He told me
The beach the bars
Him and four mates and
I can still go if I want to
I think on
With not
A skerrick of doubt
Count me out.

And Jeff and Rosy
Invite us to accompany them
With two other lovely couples
On a hugely discounted 10-day
Cruise around Pacific Islands.

And
We are requested
To be at
The monthly dinner
Held by Mr and Mrs Duckworth
On the 22nd
And it's only
Seven days away and
I'm rapidly running out
Of different ways
To say
No, we can't make it.

And
We are almost
Insulted and
Verbally bludgeoned
Because we
Didn't attend
The latest twilight social bowls tournament at which
All the local gossips gather.

And
We showed no enthusiasm
To go to
The Saturday arvo family day barbecue
Where there would be
Half the local footy team
And their footy fanatic housewives
And revheads and Acca Dacca fans and
A million kids.
And our next-door neighbour
Repeatedly demands
You must come
To the next function at our church
A free dinner, pop music
And everybody will be your friend.

And, this takes the double cream cake
A complimentary ticket invitation
(regular cost about two weeks of pension)
To the V8 car racing gig
That includes an after-race show
By a third-grade scream and bash rock 'n' roll band
That is
Surely
My kind of hell.

Some of us
Just don't go for
These popular events.

Some of us
Are just born that way.

Sorry

Sorry…
The new phenomenon sweeping the world
Don't know when it started
Don't know how it started
But it's sure caught on.

The most horrendous, cruel, brutal acts occur
Some time later
Someone says sorry
The most despicable, deliberate deeds
Of conning and thieving take place
A few months later
Someone says sorry
To make it all okay.

Go on boys
Do what you want
Tell all those lies
Perpetuate the cover up
Destroy peoples lives
Blow up the civilians
Abuse the children
Rob us of life savings
Whatever you choose
Just as long as you later front up
To the confession session
Say sorry
And make it all okay.

Frozen

Time
Time
Time
Sometimes the most beautiful thing
That awful, heartbreaking event
Of 10, 20, 30 years ago
Now frozen into the past
Dormant
A freeze frame, a single image
Is what remains
Sealing in all the raw emotion
That then had you
Reeling and desperate
Now set in ice
In the past.

Time
Sets you free of it.

Now He's Gone

You kept on saying
He drives me mad
I wish he'd go out
That'll make me glad
One of his long boating trips or
Spend more time at
The men's shed
Go overseas with all his pals
And I could see you thinking
Maybe even find a new romance
He's not the man I married
He used to make me laugh.

Forty-something years
You've been together
Shared your living, your love
Your eating
Your dancing
Your sleeping
Your sorrow and grief.

I said, half in jest
Be careful
What you're wishing for, Janice
Everything comes and
Everything goes.

Now
You're inconsolable
He had a pain
You thought would go away
He had a pain
You'd never planned for
It brought him down
And now he's gone.
Is this what you wanted, all along
You sit at home
Can't play his favourite song
All the time feeling you have
Nowhere to belong.

You never thought
What it would be like
Now that he's gone.

Memories

She says, 'But you have the memories'

I did it all
Had loved ones
Opportunities
Lived it to the full
Was blessed
Lucky
Spoilt
Loved.

They're memories
Only memories
All the people gone
All the places far away.

Memories are
Cardboard cutouts
Inanimate
Pasted
Onto
Your mind's sky.

The Operating Theatre

Entering
Is into another world
Deep in the heart of the building
An exclusive little place
Peace, but quietly buzzing
The silent hum of expensive equipment
Lights and beeps
In the room with no windows.

I lay there, prepared
I'm the main attraction
The centre
Of this tiny world
All the mundane
And trivialities
Left outside.

Care for each other
Care for each other
And I must remember to organise
That party of all parties sometime soon.

The nurses…
Angels with face masks
The surgeon…
God, the main man
With my life in his hands.

Nervous, though calm
A final thought:
Seconds to go
To oblivion…

And back?

DV

Here in the lucky country
There's an outbreak
Epidemic
Of men
Beating up women
Men
Killing women.

Domestic Violence, DV the category
Like an industry
Slotting into society's agenda
Domestic violence victims
Domestic violence perpetrators
Domestic violence leave
DV Education Course seminars
An Anti-Domestic Violence campaigner Australian of the Year
And so on.

All kinds of men
Indulge in this pursuit
Young men, old men
The very presentable businessman
The overpaid footballer
Foreign men
Aboriginal men
The good old regular Aussie bloke
In this, the lucky country
A fair go, and all that.

It's more prevalent here
Than almost anywhere else in the first world
Why is this?
In our lucky egalitarian nation
Of prosperity
Sunshine
Equal opportunity
Multicultural blending
Diversity
And all manner of equality mantras.

Does one dare to think
That this abundance
Of all things
This freedom and greed
This mix and match society
The fair go slogan – merely a cliché?
Economic growth at any cost
The overbearing censorship, restriction, regulation
Are contributing factors
To this
Detestable situation?

Not Making Sense

Contemplating lighting up
Another cigarette
For once I read
The warning on the pack:
It will kill me.
Quitting today
Will reduce the risk
Of this
Of that
And everything else.

I pause a moment
And say 'bollocks'
Place it between my lips
Ignite it and go –
Ah, it's lovely.

I know the risks
I know it's filthy
I know the government
Have put a stop
To me retreating to the veranda
Of my honeymoon restaurant
And relaxing to the sheer pleasure I get
From a smoke
Whilst sharing a glass of wine
Some sweet talk
And sitting beneath the moonlight
With my wife…
One of the kindest people
I've ever known.

Home and Away

We used to embrace
Used to talk, play, face to face
Now I'm just remembering
Just thinking, over here
In a far away place.

Another moonlight rising
Over the Serpentine calm
Would be something to behold
Another cup of coffee
On the pier at Great Yarmouth
Would be wonderful
Before we get too old.

Merrymaking on the grass
With a whisky in deepest winter
Is a memory I can't get
Out of my head.

Though you're not here
Not around
I've never forgotten
All the things we did and said.

Clinging to pictures, the era, the age
Clinging to moments in time
I have home sickness, away sickness
Write poems and songs
For the people and places I pine.

My life in pieces
My life in halves
Nothing
Prepares one
For a life
Of two seasons.

Urban Bourbon and Beer

Went to the 4 o'clock
Snacks and booze
Suburban neighbourhood get together yesterday
And the grating vibes
From the intercourse
Still jangles my
Nervous system.

Sit that end, Dougie
With the men
She
Can be with the girls.

Sometimes it's very tough
Not having control
Never been a man's man
And 'she'
Never been a girl's girl.

It's all so presumptuously friendly
They've found me out
I'm not in their league
Out of my tree
Out of my depth
The judgements are crushing
My mission to be
An interesting mystery
Has failed.

Thank you
This morning
For the serene
Solitude
Of sunrise.

Things I'll Never Know

You have a new intimacy
He didn't seem your type
But I take the liberty
I know what you like.

Did you pick up on the things
We always liked to do
Fun days shopping at the market
Seeking out a bargain or two
Cuddling in the back row of a movie show and
Drinking black beer on the end of the bed
Prolonging the desire
Whilst playing *Talking Heads*
Stroking your back, licking your face
Do you loiter in our favourite place
Does he get the same tingles when you wear your black dress
The one embroidered with the see-through lace
Do you get a mutual pleasure from sitting on the deck
Taking in a nature show
Or is it all different now…
The things I'll never know.

He doesn't seem your type
So grown up and mature
He reminds me of your father
Is that what you're looking for?
What is it you do together and where do you go
Your longing for a different life
The things I'll never know.

I look onwards today
Little point in thinking past
But you're still here in the afterglow
Were you only truth by half?

Sebastian

Sebastian is an amiable chap
Somewhat worldly, adroit
Cluey, classless, clear.

Bewilderingly
He has very few friends
Even, I would say, none.
He is seemingly
Sociable, generous, informal
Likes to lead, be led
Likes to talk, listen
Takes advice and
Is well read.

Sebastian likes to say,
'People often don't like me'
I thought:
Why not, they're mad.
Sebastian is the sort of man
You'd be pleased to have as
A friend
A colleague
A brother.
So, I'm moved
To commence an investigation.

Perhaps Sebastian is
A man on the outside
With the real man disguised
Hidden
On the inside.

You could tell Sebastian anything
In confidence
And be sure
It is kept locked away.

Soon enough
Down the track a little
Belinda
Whom I call the brat
Would describe something to me
In perfect detail
And crude around the edges
Of a time, a happening
That only I
And Sebastian
Knew of.

My head in a whirl
I continue my research.

Sebastian betrays confidences and
Other things come to light.
Sebastian has a secret life
A double life.
He employs young boys
To do his maintenance, gardening
Community-minded and kindly with payment
But Sebastian likes to watch them work
Shirtless and in little shorts.

Sebastian has a concealed room
In his house
That no one's allowed to enter.
I thought it contained
Knowledge and wisdom
Because I thought Sebastian was my mentor.
But he panicked and broke down
When his house was burgled
And some secret things were stolen.

Sebastian 'forgets'
The commitments he made
Takes the phone off the hook
Trusts time
To make them fade.

How blinded have I been?
How naïve?
If Sebastian hadn't told me
That people don't like him
I would never have seen him in his shadow.

Sarah Ann

You've left, Mum
It's finally over
I wasn't there this week
Didn't fly back
Funerals are grotesque affairs
Got sent a DVD
There was a bits and pieces family representation
No eldest son, your love child
No youngest son
No husbands
The master of ceremony
Almost
Making you out to be someone unrecognisable
And I'm living here
With my ups and downs
My night in your cold, dark winter day
Tears frozen
In the upside down bit of the world.

You always welcomed me back
With open loving arms
And loving unconditional
That's why I love you
That's what I'll miss.

I saw what they did
I heard what they said
It's only the truth that counts
You're innocent
You're free.

You're love
You're innocent
That
Is what
I'll miss.

Hit Parade

Pop song titles inspiring new stories

The following poems were inspired by pop song titles
(the poems do not relate to the lyrics of the original songs):
My Sweet Lord (George Harrison, 1971)
If Not For You (Bob Dylan,1970)
Avalanche (Leonard Cohen, 1971)
Stop (Sam Brown, 1988)
The Other Guy (Little River Band, 1982)
Honesty (Billy Joel, 1978)
Yesterday (Beatles, 1965)
Another Tear Falls (Walker Brothers, 1966)
Waiting For the Miracle (Leonard Cohen, 1992)
Little Things (Dave Berry, 1965)
Liar Liar (Castaways, 1965)
Hit and Miss (John Barry Orchestra, 1960)
Good Vibrations (Beach Boys, 1966)
I Should Have Known Better (Beatles, 1964)
Alone Again Or (Love, 1967)
I love You Because (Jim Reeves, 1964)

My Sweet Lord

Coming home in the car
On the radio they play
'My Sweet Lord'.
Nothing encapsulates the era
The washed-up hippie years
More than this song.
I increase the volume
To four
No more
To six
The booming base line
The chorus crescendo
The magical key changes
Fills the car, my head and
My whole body vibrates as it plays through.
I feel just as, I imagine, a 17-year-old P-plater would
Belting out his new favourite rap track
In his new-found freedom.
This is my song, my music, from my age
And it fills me with a passion
And excitement.

I loved you George
Always out there searching
Just as I was
Checking out Jesus, Buddha and
All that other mystical Eastern stuff
Though I never saw it
Never found it
I've always held on
To the desire
For all encompassing love
And peace
And justice
And togetherness.
This song, 'My Sweet Lord'
From half a century ago
Playing out in the car
At break-point volume
Filling me with nostalgia
Was the beginning
And end
To my search for
A supreme being.

If Not For You

I have an Aboriginal friend
Mixed-race Australian/European
An activist, campaigner for rights
And I detect
The bitterness
That stems
From the invasion.
I share her view.

Conscious of not wanting to appear
To play down
The enormous consequence
Of the big issue
I,
Being me,
True to nature
Cherish life
Always looking for a positive
Suggested that
Just for a moment
Look at the
Smaller picture
Personally
If not for the invasion
Jessie
You would not have
Been born
And we wouldn't know each other.

It makes nothing right and,
Makes nothing wrong.
This is
As it is.

Avalanche

A former friend of mine
Once inspired me to
Feel free
To write
To socialise
To drink red wine
Have fun
To cherish the day –
His favourite cliché
To trust a little more
To be positive
To believe in friendship
To see the good
Above the bad
To be appreciative and grateful
For all that I have
I trusted his word
His sentiments
His deeds
I trusted him to
Be alone with my wife.

He an educated man
With a respectable, high status
Responsible job
Very presentable, well spoken with
A vast vocabulary.
He listened and encouraged
Liked my music
Was never in a hurry.

I've written about him before
Back in two thousand and four.

One little spark
Caused an avalanche.
Everything unravelled
Soft sand turned to gravel.
Nothing was believable
Good intertwined with evil.

Inevitably came
The final blow
Disbelief
Demoralising
How could it go so low.

And every day, or week, or month
A contrary truth is realised.
He is a former friend of mine.

Stop

Everything's glowing and
I feel great
Your eyes are sparkling
Don't let it abate.

Stop
The moment
I want to
Stay here
Forever.

The Other Guy

Just open
Your blouse
To him
My love
Please not
Your heart
As well.

Honesty

I'm not partial
To liars
But
Have to deal with my own hypocrisy
Because
I feign a lot and
Justify it.
I feign myopia
When I don't want my path to cross with
Certain persons
I feign laughter
When the expectation is
To laugh
At a stupid joke
I feign toughness
When I don't want the slightly acquainted
Macho fellas at the bar
To think I'm weak
I feign interest
When people harp on about
Their children, their Bali holiday
Or the guys who talk incessantly about cars
I feign self-confidence
When I don't want to expose my fragility
I feign surprise
When told something I already know
And wasn't supposed to

I feign forgetfulness
When it is the only excuse I can muster
For letting someone down, or,
In severe cases
Even hint at the early stage of dementia
And I feign agreement
In a palm away manner
When my views are opposed to others.

I've feigned all of this
Since I was very young
I've had to
Just to 'keep in'
Due to the fear
Of being a total misfit
Outcast
So am quite adept at it
Adept also at seeing
Other people feign.

But
I cannot feign tears
I have at least
That much pride and honesty
To ensure
I stay true to myself.

Yesterday

I try to grasp your hands
But they merely limp away
A hug
Is greeted with
A shuffle, a shrug
To 'happy new year' you respond
As a parrot does to passers-by
Memories of our last encounter
Keep on flooding back
Offensive and abusive atrocious behaviour
Left with nothing to remind you
Nothing to savour
All the rules of everything
Can go to bloody hell.

If only
Our eyes would meet
And we could share again
A tiny bit
Of yesterday.

Another Tear Falls

Lying here
Chilling on the lawn
My creaky body still with me
Still
The same old sun
Warming me
As it did when I was young
When the time was full
Of hope and fun.

We were all so energetic
Creative
Looking forward
But living for then.
All the love and belief
Beautiful music
Flowers and peace
Echoes down the years.

I see in the sky
The images of
Arthur Lee, Jerry Garcia
Grace Slick and Donovan
Joan Baez, Neil Young, Crosby
Beefheart, John Lennon, Country Joe
Where did all those messages go
We wanted the world to heed
And today
Another tear falls
For the departing
Of Leonard Cohen.

What are you doing right now
Those of you still with us
Adjusting your recliner
Waiting for the bell
That calls you to the diner
Tending the blooms and vegies
Being cared for, reminiscing
Still full of light
Making music for the new generation
Thinking of your next incarnation.

Do you wonder
Why it all came down
Disappeared without a sound
Did you know
When it was the final show?

And time, of course
Takes us all
But we never did have
The final call.

Waiting for the Miracle

The party
Had a large gathering
Boisterous
Drunk
Menacing
Every story, statement, comment
Brought loud hearty party laughter.

I wasn't impressed
Interested
Inebriated
Nor particularly sociable
Though I persevered
Hoping for some kind of breakthrough
Waiting for a miracle.

Some chap asked me
If I was OK
I said sure, fine
He didn't believe me
And took to forceful, bullying
Persuasion
To 'get into the spirit' and
Join in
He said
'You take yourself too seriously, mate'

I thought
If I don't care
For the conversations
The bigotry
The boorish
Don't share the same
Narrow-minded views
Don't find the jesting very funny
How much
Should I
Compromise myself
To appear happy?

Little Things

It's a beautiful day
I love it
And then the battle
Always there to be fought
Of minor irritants and petty details
I have to brush aside
To get to the end of the day.

Little things
Like maybe an excruciatingly crass front-page headline
On my newspaper
A dead car struck animal
In the gutter
Meeting with a dull gossipy acquaintance
During my morning stroll
A neighbour
Screaming at his dog
He won't allow on the lawn
My local member of the senate announcing that
'God will guide my decisions'
The sound of chainsaws
In the main street removing trees
To make way for more parking lots
The sight of the lake murky
Contaminated
Lifeless

The thought of my visit to
The dentist
He's looking to bolster up his
Spending fund
For the 21-day European cruise
And a car sticker advising,
Australia: if you don't love it
FUCK OFF.
Little things.

It's lunchtime
I sit down to
Melted cheese on toast
And consider the
Big things
In life.

Liar Liar

Lies lies lies
Liars everywhere
The world is abundant with liars
History is full of liars
Make you helpless, hopeless
Broken-hearted, angry.

Husbands lie to wives
The bank clerk
Lies to customers
From the top to the bottom
Governments lie to its people
Supermarkets lie to consumers
The church lies to its parishioners
The rich lie to the poor
The salesman lies
Advertising lies
The politician pulls the wool over our eyes
The prosecution lie to the jury
Mining companies lie
To landowners
Everyday
It's in your face
The priest lies
And lies and lies
A pope lies
And is made a saint
The Vatican is a lie

The prime minister
and his ministers
Are serial liars
The millionaires lie
To the tax department
The war-crazed Germans
Lied to the French
The French lied to the Jews
The missionaries lied to the natives
The British lied
To children sent to the colonies
The Americans lie to the world.

I'm left to ponder:
If there were no lies
Could we bear the truth?

Hit and Miss

What possibly…

It would never have been the same
If only I'd caught that train.

Good Vibrations

Some people give themselves
Good lives
Wonderful lives
Everything's on the up
Humour to be found everywhere
Positive vibrations.

I have a friend who
Is precisely this
His smile settled
Real and true
His laughter comes right out at you
Like heat from fire.

I admire him
He's a gas to be around
Everyone enjoys being
His friend.

Not always politically correct but
No one takes offence
He's old-fashioned
Not come to terms
With all the new words.

I study him
Analyse him
He's constant
Never gets a cold
Does not seem old
Never feels threatened
Walking along lowly lit suburban side streets
Greets all with the same
Open warmth and welcome
He's had his down times
But my friend lets life happen
And so, mostly, comes through unscathed.

In contrast
I give myself a hard life
Greet people with suspicion
My self-doubt is
My armour, my ammunition
It governs everything.

In my imaginary world
I trade places with him
For a brief time
And try
Just to let
Life happen.

I Should Have Known Better

The move to the suburbs
It didn't work out
The experiment failed
Always trying to fit in
Always trying to hold on
I should have known better
With a mind like mine.

Don't know where I'm at
Don't know what I want
I Just can't ease in to the norm
Everywhere that's settled
And I make my moves
I tip the balance
Turn it into a storm.

There's another place somewhere
Though I don't know where
That's maybe where I want to live
But I should have known better
Than to move to the suburbs
Where I feel there is nothing to give.

Alone Again Or

Becoming seventy
It's mind-boggling
'Having a party, Doug?'
I think not
Just quietly see it through
Spend the time with You.

I never thought I'd reach
This milestone
As a young hippie
We never wanted to be that old generation
Whom mostly despised us
And whom we
Wanted to replace
With a new agenda
Of love and flowers and peace.

Now,
We've all become our parents, our grandparents
Dispersed
Throughout the world
Alone with the dreams
The flowers growing today
Being readied for our graves.
Many cling to some faith and
Look forward to
Uniting with their god
So as to never
Be
Alone.

I don't have such delusions or expectations
We are all alone
From birth
We have attachments
And detachments
Cling to this person, or that person
And let go

We cling to family, wealth and books
And let go
To things and ideals
To health and looks
And let go
We cling to life itself
Then let go.

The only time
We're not alone
Is when
We're in
The womb.

I Love You Because

I love you.
Often overcome
By this emotion
Not confined to
One person or one place
One activity or one prize
One sunset or moonrise
One morning, one night
One darkness, one light.
It rests, dormant
Then rises.
I love my wife
For her boundless giving
I love my mother for just living
I love my body
For keeping me going
My open mind that lets me keep seeing
My heart, that keeps on ticking
I love my best mate
For just being
I love my first love
Who's always made me feel worthy
I love my car
When it delivers me safely
My dog
Who always forgives me
When I don't take her walking on time

I love my doctor
When he tells me don't worry, you're fine
My dentist when I'm paying and saying goodbye
After he's fixed my aching teeth
For the one-hundredth time
I love a green politician
For sharing my passion
And, I love the words
That come
From my longing.

www.ingramcontent.com/pod-product-compliance
Lightning Source LLC
Chambersburg PA
CBHW070937080526
44589CB00013B/1548